The Poetry of Aphra Behn

Volume II – A Miscellany of Poems

Aphra Behn was a prolific and well established writer but facts about her remain scant and difficult to confirm. What can safely be said though is that Aphra Behn is now regarded as a key English playwright and a major figure in Restoration theatre

Aphra was born into the rising tensions to the English Civil War. Obviously a time of much division and difficulty as the King and Parliament, and their respective forces, came ever closer to conflict.

There are claims she was a spy, that she travelled abroad, possibly as far as Surinam.

By 1664 her marriage was over (though by death or separation is not known but presumably the former as it occurred in the year of their marriage) and she now used Mrs Behn as her professional name.

Aphra now moved towards pursuing a more sustainable and substantial career and began work for the King's Company and the Duke's Company players as a scribe.

Previously her only writing had been poetry but now she would become a playwright. Her first, "The Forc'd Marriage", was staged in 1670, followed by "The Amorous Prince" (1671). After her third play, "The Dutch Lover", Aphra had a three year lull in her writing career. Again it is speculated that she went travelling again, possibly once again as a spy.

After this sojourn her writing moves towards comic works, which prove commercially more successful. Her most popular works included "The Rover" and "Love-Letters Between a Nobleman and His Sister" (1684–87).

With her growing reputation Aphra became friends with many of the most notable writers of the day. This is The Age of Dryden and his literary dominance.

From the mid 1680's Aphra's health began to decline. This was exacerbated by her continual state of debt and descent into poverty.

Aphra Behn died on April 16th 1689, and is buried in the East Cloister of Westminster Abbey. The inscription on her tombstone reads: "Here lies a Proof that Wit can never be Defence enough against Mortality." She was quoted as stating that she had led a "life dedicated to pleasure and poetry."

Index of Contents

WESTMINSTER DROLLERY, 1671.
A SONG.
MISCELLANY, 1685.
To SIR WILLIAM CLIFTON
MISCELLANY, 1685.
On the Death of the late Earl of Rochester
SONG By A. B.
A SONG by Mrs. A. B.
A PARAPHRASE on the LORDS PRAYER. By Mrs. A. B.
SELINDA and CLORIS, made in an Entertainment at Court. By Mrs. A. B.
A PINDARIC to Mr. P. who sings finely.
On the Author of that Excellent Book Intituled The Way to Health, Long Life, and Happiness
Epitaph on the Tombstone of a Child, the last of Seven that died before.
Epilogue to the Jealous Lovers. 1682.
A PASTORAL to Mr. Stafford, Under the Name of SILVIO on his Translation of the Death of Camilla: out of VIRGIL.
GILDON'S MISCELLANY, 1692.
Verses design d by Mrs. A. Behn to be sent to a fair Lady, that desired she would absent herself to cure her Love. Left unfinished.
Verses by Madam Behn, never before printed. On a Conventicle.
GILDON'S CHORUS POETARUM, 1694.
MUSES MERCURY, June, 1707.
The Complaint of the poor Cavaliers.
On a Pin that hurt Amintas' Eye.
To Mrs. Harsenet, on the Report of a Beauty which she went to see at Church.
For Damon, being ask'd a Reason for his Love.
FAMILIAR LETTERS, 1718.
A Letter to the Earl of Kildare, dissuading him from marrying Moll Howard.
To Mrs. Price.
P. S. A SONG.
PROLOGUE to ROMULUS,
EPILOGUE to the Same.
Mrs. Behn's Satyr on Dryden.
(On Mr. Dryden, Renegate.)
VALENTINIAN. Prologue spoken by Mrs. Cook the first Day.
To Henry Higden, Esq; on his Translation of the Tenth Satyr of Juvenal.
On the Death of E. Waller, Esq;
A PINDARIC POEM to the Reverend Doctor Burnet, on the Honour he did me of Enquiring after me and my MUSE.
APHRA BEHN – A SHORT BIOGRAPHY
APHRA BEHN – A CONCISE BIBLIOGRAPHY

On the Honourable Sir Francis Fane, on his Play caird the Sacrifice, by Mrs. A. B.

Long have our Priests condemned a wicked Age,
And every little criticks sensless rage
Damn'd a forsaken self-declining stage:
Great 'tis confest and many are our crimes,
And no less profligate the vitious times,

But yet no wonder both prevail so ill,
The Poets fury and the Preachers skill;
While to the World it is so plainly known
They blame our faults with great ones of their own,
Let their dull Pens flow with unlearned spight
And weakly censure what the skilful write;
You, learned Sir, a nobler passion shew,
Our best of rules and best example too.
Precepts and grave instructions dully move,
The brave Performer better do's improve,
Ver'st in the truest Satyr you excel
And shew how ill we write by writing well.
This noble Piece which well deserves your name
I read with pleasure tho I read with shame.
The tender Laurels which my brows had drest
Flag, like young Flowers, with too much heat opprest.
The generous fire I felt in every line
Shew'd me the cold, the feeble, force of mine.
Henceforth Tie you for imitation chuse
Your nobler flights will wing my Callow Muse;
So the young Eagle is inform'd to fly
By seeing the Monarch Bird ascend the sky.
And tho with less success her strength she'l try,
Spreads her soft plumes and his vast tracks persues
Tho far above the towring Prince she views:
High as she can she'll bear your deathless fame,
And make my song Immortal by your name.
But where the work is so Divinely wrought,
The rules so just and so sublime each thought,
When with so strict an Art your scenes are plac'd
With wit so new, and so uncommon, grac'd,
In vain, alas! I should'st attempt to tell
Where, or in what, your Muse do's most excel.
Each character performs its noble part,
And stamps its Image on the Readers heart.

In Tamer Ian you a true Hero drest,
A generous conflict wars within his breast,
This there the mightyest passions you have shew'd
By turns confest the Mortal and the God.
When e're his steps approach the haughty fair
He bows indeed but like a Conqueror,
Compell'd to Love yet scorns his servial chain,
In spight of all you make the Monarch reign.
But who without resistless tears can see
The bright, the innocent, Irene die?
Axallcfs life a noble ransom paid,
In vain to save the much-lov'd charming maid,
Nought surely cou'd but your own flame inspire
Your happy Muse to reach so soft a fire.
Yet with what Art you turn the pow'rful stream

When trecherous Ragallzan is the theam:
You mix our different passions with such skill,
We feel 'em all and all with pleasure feel.
We love the mischief, tho the harms we grieve,
And for his wit the villain we forgive.
In your Despina all those passions meet,
Which womans frailties perfectly compleat.
Pride and Revenge, Ambition, Love and Rage,
At once her wilful haughty Soul engage;
And while her rigid Honour we esteem,
The dire effects as justly must condemn.
She shews a virtue so severely nice
As has betray'd it to a pitch of vice.
All which confess a God-like pow'r in you
Who cou'd form woman to herself so true.

Live, mighty Sir, to reconcile the Age
To the first glories of the useful Stage.
'Tis you her rifl'd Empire may restore
[And give her power she ne're cou'd boast before.

To Damon.

To inquire of him if be cou'd tell me by the Style, who writ me a Copy of Verses that came to me in an unknown Hand.

Oh, Damon, if thou ever wert
That certain friend thou hast profest,
Relieve the Pantings of my heart,
Restore me to my wonted rest.
Late in the Silvian Grove I sat,
Free as the Air, and calm as that;
For as no winds the boughs opprest,
No storms of Love were in my breast.
A long Adieu I'd bid to that
Ere since Amintas prov'd ingrate.
And with indifference, or disdain,
I lookt around upon the Plain
And worth my favor found no sighing Swain.
But oh, my Damon, all in vain
I triumph'd in security,
In vain absented from the Plain.
The wanton God his power to try
In lone recesses makes us yeild,
As well as in the open feild;
For where no human thing was found
My heedless heart receiv'd a wound.
Assist me, Shepherd, or I dye,
Help to unfold this Mystery.

No Swain was by, no flattering Nymph was neer,
Soft tales of Love to whisper in my Ear.
In sleep, no Dream my fancy fir'd
With Images, my waking wish desir'd.
No fond Idea fill'd my mind;
Nor to the faithless sex one thought inclin'd;
I sigh'd for no deceiving youth,
Who forfeited his vows and truth;
I waited no Assigning Swain
Whose disappointment gave me pain.
My fancy did no prospect take
Of Conquest's I designed to make.
No snares for Lovers I had laid,
Nor was of any snare afraid.
But calm and innocent I sate,
Content with my indifferent fate.
(A Medium, I confess, I hate.)
For when the mind so cool is grown
As neither Love nor Hate to own,
The Life but dully lingers on.

Thus in the mid'st of careless thought,
A paper to my hand was brought.
What hidden charms were lodg'd within,
To my unwary Eyes unseen,
Alas! no Human thought can guess;
But ho! it robb'd me of my peace.
A Philter 'twas, that darted pain
Thro every pleas'd and trembling vein.
A stratagem, to send a Dart
By a new way into the heart,
Th' Ignoble Policie of Love
By a clandestin means to move.
Which possibly the Instrument
Did ne're design to that intent,
But only form, and complement.
While Love did the occasion take
And hid beneath his flowres a snake,
O're every line did Poyson fling,
In every word he lurk't a sting.
So Matrons are, by Demons charms,

Tho harmless, capable of harms.
The verse was smooth, the thought was fine,
The fancy new, the wit divine.
But fill'd with praises of my face and Eyes,
My verse, and all those usual flatteries
To me as common as the Air;
Nor cou'd my vanity procure my care.
All which as things of course are writ

And less to shew esteem than wit.
But here was some strange somthing more
Than ever flatter'd me before;
My heart was by my Eyes misled:
I blusht and trembl'd as I read.
And every guilty look confest
I was with new surprise opprest.
From every view I felt a pain
And by the Soul, I drew the Swain.
Charming as fancy cou'd create
Fine as his Poem, and as soft as that.
I drew him all the heart cou'd move,
I drew him all that women Love.
And such a dear Idea made
As has my whole repose betray 'd.
Pigmalion thus his Image form'd,
And for the charms he made, he sigh'd and burn'd,

Oh thou that know'st each Shepherds Strains
That Pipes and Sings upon the Plains;
Inform me where the youth remains.
The spightful Paper bare no name,
Nor can I guess from whom it came,
Or if at least a guess I found,
'Twas not t'instruct but to confound.

To Alexis in Answer to His Poem against Fruition. Ode

Ah hapless sex! who bear no charms,
But what like lightning flash and are no more,
False fires sent down for baneful harms,
Fires which the fleeting Lover feebly warms
And given like past Beboches o're,
Like Songs that please (tho bad,) when new,
But learn'd by heart neglected grew.

In vain did Heav'n adorn the shape and face
With Beautyes which by Angels forms it drew:
In vain the mind with brighter Glories Grace,
While all our joys are stinted to the space
Of one betraying enterview,
With one surrender to the eager will
We 're short-liv'd nothing, or a real ill.

Since Man with that inconstancy was born,
To love the absent, and the present scorn,
Why do we deck, why do we dress
For such a short-liv'd happiness?
Why do we put Attraction on,

Since either way tis we must be undon?

They fly if Honour take our part,
Our Virtue drives 'em o're the field.
We lose 'em by too much desert,
And Oh! they fly us if we yeild.
Ye Gods! is there no charm in all the fair
To fix this wild, this faithless, wanderer?

Man! our great business and our aim,
For whom we spread our fruitless snares,
No sooner kindles the designing flame,
But to the next bright object bears
The Trophies of his conquest and our shame:
Inconstancy's the good supream
The rest is airy Notion, empty Dream!
Then, heedless Nymph, be rul'd by me
If e're your Swain the bliss desire;
Think like Alexis he may be
Whose wisht Possession damps his fire;
The roving youth in every shade
Has left some sighing arid abandon'd Maid,
For tis a fatal lesson he has learn'd,
After fruition ne're to be concern'd.

To Alexis, On his saying, I lov'd a Man that talk'd much

Alexis, since you'l have it so
I grant I am impertinent.
And till this moment did not know
Thro all my life what 'twas I merit;
Your kind opinion was th' unflattering Glass,
In which my mind found how defonn'd it was.

In your clear sense which knows no art,
I saw the error of my Soul;
And all the feebless of my heart,
With one reflection you controul,
Kind as a God, and gently you chastise,
By what you hate, you teach me to be wise.

Impertinence, my sexes shame,
(Which has so long my life persu'd,)
You with such modesty reclaim
As all the Woman has subdu'd,
To so divine a power what must I owe,
That renders me so like the perfect you?

That conversable thing I hate

Already with a just disdain,
Who Prid's himself upon his prate
And is of word, (that Nonsense,) vain;
When in your few appears such excellence,
They have reproacht, and charm'd me into sense.

For ever may I listning sit,
Tho but each hour a word be born:
I wou'd attend the coming wit,
And bless what can so well inform:
Let the dull World henceforth to words be damn'd,
I'm into nobler sense than talking sham'd.

A PASTORAL PINDARICK

On the Marriage of the Right Honourable the Earle of Dorset and Midlesex, to the Lady Mary Compton.

A Dialogue. Between Damon and Aminta.

Aminta
Whither, young Damon, whither in such hast,
Swift as the Winds you sweep the Grove,
The Amorous God of Day scarce hy'd so fast
After his flying Love?

Damon
Aminta, view my Face, and thence survey
My very Soul and all its mighty joy!
A joy too great to be conceal'd,
And without speaking is reveal'd
For this eternal Holyday.
A Day to place i'th' Shepherds Kalendar,
To stand the glory of the circling year.
Let it's blest date on every Bark be set,
And every Echo its dear name repeat.
Let 'em tell all the neighbouring Woods and Plains,
That Lysidus, the Beauty of the Swains,
Our darling youth, our wonder and our Pride,
Is blest with fair Clemena for a Bride.
Oh happy Pair! Let all the Groves rejoyce,
And gladness fill each heart and every voyce!

Aminta
Clemena! that bright maid for whom our Shepherds pine,
For whom so many weeping Eyes decline!
For whom the Echos all complain,
For whom with sigh and falling tears
The Lover in his soft despairs

Disturbs the Peaceful Rivers gliding stream?
The bright Clemena who has been so long
The destinie of hearts and yet so young,
She that has robb'd so many of content
Yet is herself so Sweet, so Innocent.
She, that as many hearts invades,
As charming Lysidus has conquer'd maids,
Oh tell me, Damon, is the lovely fair
Become the dear reward of all the Shepherds care?
Has Lysidus that prize of Glory won
For whom so many sighing Swains must be undon?

Damon
Yes, it was destin'd from Eternity,
They only shou'd each other's be,
Hail, lovely pair, whom every God design'd
In your first great Creation shou'd be joyn'd.

Aminta
Oh, Damon, this is-vain Philosophic,
'Tis chance and not Divinity,
That guides Loves Partial Darts;
And we in vain the Boy implore
To make them Love whom we Adore.
And all the other powers take little care of hearts,
The very Soule's by intr'est sway'd,
And nobler passion now by fortune is betray'd;
By sad experience this I know,
And sigh, Alas! in vain because tis true.

Damon
Too often and too fatally we find
Portion and Joynture charm the mind,
Large Flocks and Herds, and spacious Plains
Becoms the merit of the Swains.
But here, tho both did equally abound,
'T was youth, 'twas wit, 'twas Beauty gave the equal wound;
Their Soules were one before they mortal being found.
Jove when he layd his awful Thunder by
And all his softest Attributes put on,
When Heav'n was Gay, and the vast Glittering Sky
With Deities all wondering and attentive shone,
The God his Lucky est heat to try
Form'd their great Soules of one Immortal Ray,
He thought, and form'd, as first he did the World,
But with this difference, That from Chaos came,
These from a beam, which, from his God-head hurl'd
Kindl'd into an everlasting flame.
He smiling saw the mighty work was good,
While all the lesser Gods around him gazing stood.
He saw the shining Model bright and Great

But oh! they were not yet compleat,
For not one God but did the flames inspire,
With sparks of their Divinest fire.

Diana took the lovely Female Soul,
And did its fiercer Atoms cool;
Softn'd the flame and plac'd a Chrystal Ice
About the sacred Paradise,
Bath'd it all or'e in Virgin Tears,
Mixt with the fragrant Dew the Rose receives,
Into the bosom of her untoucht leaves,
And dry'd it with the breath of Vestal Prayers,
Juno did great Majestick thought inspire
And Pallas toucht it with Heroick fire.

While Mars, Apollo, Love and Venus sate,
About the Hero's Soul in high debate,
Each claims it all, but all in vain contend,
In vain appeal to mighty Jove,
Who equal Portions did to all extend.
This to the God of wit, and that to Love,
Another to the Queen of soft desire,
And the fierce God of War compleats the rest,
Guilds it all or'e with Martial fire;
While Love, and Wit, Beauty and War exprest
Their finest Arts, and the bright Beings all in Glory drest.

While each in their Divine imployments strove
By every charm these new-form'd lights t'improve,
They left a space untoucht for mightyer Love.
The finishing last strokes the Boy perform'd;
Who from his Quiver took a Golden Dart
That cou'd a sympathizing wound impart,
And toucht 'em both, and with one flame they burn'd.
The next great work was to create two frames
Of the Divinest form,
Fit to contain these heavenly flames.
The Gods decreed, and charming Lysidus was born,
Born, and grew up the wonder of the Plains,
Joy of the Nymphs and Glory of the Swains.
And warm'd all hearts with his inchanting strains;
Soft were the Songs, which from his lips did flow,
Soft as the Soul which the fine thought conceiv'd.
Soft as the sighs the charming Virgin breath'd
The first dear night of the chast nuptial vow.
The noble youth even Daphnis do's excel,
Oh never Shepherd pip'd and sung so well.

Aminta
Now, Damon, you are in your proper sphear,
While of his wit you give a character.

But who inspired you a Philosopher?

Damon
Old Colin, when we oft have led our Flocks
Beneath the shelter of the shad's and Rocks,
While other youths more vainly spent their time,
I listen'd to the wonderous Bard;
And while he sung of things sublime
With reverend pleasure heard.
He soar'd to the Divine abodes
And told the secrets of the Gods.
And oft discours'd of Love and Sympathy;
For he as well as thou and I
Had sigh't for some dear object of desire;
But oh! till now I ne're cou'd prove
That secret mystery of Love;
Ne're saw two hearts thus burn with equal fire.

Aminta
But, oh! what Nymph e're saw the noble youth
That was not to eternal Love betray'd

Damon
And, oh! what swain e're saw the Lovely maid,
That wou'd not plight her his eternal faith!
Not unblown Roses, or the new-born day
Or pointed Sun-beams, when they gild the skys,
Are half so sweet, are half so bright and gay,
As young Clements charming Face and Eyes!

Amlnta
Not full-blown flowrs, when all their luster's on
Whom every bosom longs to wear,
Nor the spread Glories of the mid-days sun
Can with the charming Lysidus compare.

Damon
Not the soft gales of gentle breez
That whisper to the yeilding Trees,
Nor songs of Birds that thro the Groves rejoyce,
Are half so sweet, so soft, as young Clements voyce.

Aminta
Not murmurs of the Rivulets and Springs,
When thro the glades they purling glide along
And listen when the wondrous shepherd sings,
Are half so sweet as is the Shepherds song.

Damon
Not young Diana in her eager chase
When by her careless flying Robe betray'd,

Discovering every charm and every Grace,
Has more surprising Beauty than the brighter maid.

Aminta
The gay young Monarch of the cheerful May
Adorn'd with all the Trophies he has won,
Vain with the Homage of the joyful day
Compared to Lysidus wou'd be undone.

Damon
Aminta, cease; and let me hast away,
For while upon this Theam you dwell,
You speak the noble youth so just, so well,
I cou'd for ever listening stay.

Aminta
And while Clements praise becoms thy choyce,
My Ravisht soul is fixt upon thy voyce.

Damon
But see the Nymphs and dancing swains
Ascend the Hill from yonder Plains,
With Wreathes and Garlands finely made,
To crown the lovely Bride and Bridegrooms head,
And I amongst the humbler throng
My Sacrifice must bring
A rural Hymeneal Song,
Alexis he shall pipe while I will sing.
Had I been blest with Flocks or Herd
A nobler Tribute I'd prepared,
With darling Lambs the Altars I wou'd throng;
But I, alas! can only offer song.
Song too obscure, too humble verse
For this days glory to reherse,
But Lysidus, like Heav'n, is kind,
And for the Sacrifice accepts the Humble mind.
If he vouchsafe to listen to my Ode
He makes me happyer than a fancy 'd God.

On Desire. A Pindarick

What Art thou, oh! thou new-found pain?
From what infection dost thou spring?
Tell me. oh! tell me, thou inchanting thing,
Thy nature, and thy name;
Inform me by what subtil Art,
What powerful Influence,
You got such vast Dominion in a part
Of my unheeded, and unguarded, heart,

That fame and Honour cannot drive yee thence.
Oh! mischievous usurper of my Peace;
Oh! soft intruder on my solitude,
Charming disturber of my ease,
Thou hast my nobler fate persu'd,
And all the Glorys of my life subdu'd.

Thou haunt'st my inconvenient hours;
The business of the Day, nor silence of the night,
That shou'd to cares and sleep invite,
Can bid defyance to thy conquering powers.
Where hast thou been this live-long Age
That from my Birth till now,
Thou never could'st one thought engage,
Or charm my soul with the uneasy rage
That made it all its humble feebles know?

Where wert thou, oh, malicious spright,
When shining Honour did invite?
When interest call'd, then thou wert shy,
Nor to my aid one kind propension brought,
Nor wou'd'st inspire one tender thought,
When Princes at my feet did lye.

When thou coud'st mix ambition with thy joy,
Then peevish Phantom thou wer't nice and coy,
Not Beauty cou'd invite thee then
Nor all the Arts of lavish Men;
Not all the powerful Rhetorick of the Tongue
Not sacred Wit cou'd charm thee on;
Not the soft play that lovers make,
Nor sigh cou'd fan thee to a fire,
Not pleading tears, nor vows cou'd thee awake,
Or warm the unform'd somthing to desire.
Oft I've conjur'd thee to appear
By youth, by love, by all their powrs,
Have searcht and sought thee every where,
In silent Groves, in lonely bowrs:
On Flowry beds where lovers wishing lye,
In sheltering woods where sighing maids
To their assigning Shepherds hye,
And hide their blushes in the gloom of shades:
Yet there, even there, tho youth assail'd,
Where Beauty prostrate lay and fortune woo'd,
My heart insensible to neither bow'd,
The lucky aid was wanting to prevail.

In courts I sought thee then, thy proper sphear
But thou in crowds wer't stifl'd there,
Int'rest did all the loving business do,
Invites the youths and wins the Virgins too.

Or if by chance some heart thy empire own
(Ah power ingrate!) the slave must be undone.

Tell me, thou nimble fire, that dost dilate
Thy mighty force thro every part,
What God, or Human power did thee create
In my, till now, unfacil heart?
Art thou some welcome plague sent from above
In this dear form, this kind disguise?
Or the false offspring of mistaken love,
Begot by some soft thought that faintly strove,
With the bright peircing Beautys of Lysanders Eyes?

Yes, yes, tormenter, I have found thee now;
And found to whom thou dost thy being owe,
'Tis thou the blushes dost impart,
For thee this languishment I wear,
'Tis thou that tremblest in my heart
When the dear Shepherd do's appear,
I faint, I dye with pleasing pain,
My words intruding sighing break
When e're I touch the charming swain
When e're I gaze, when e're I speak.
Thy conscious fire is mingl'd with my love,
As in the sanctifi'd abodes
Misguided worshippers approve
The mixing Idol with their Gods.

In vain, alas! in vain I strive
With errors, which my soul do please and vex,
For superstition will survive,
Purer Religion to perplex.

Oh! tell me you, Philosophers, in love,
That can its burning feaverish fits controul,
By what strange Arts you cure the soul,
And the fierce Calenture remove

Tell me, yee fair ones, that exchange desire,
How tis you hid the kindling fire.
Oh! wou'd you but confess the truth,
It is not real virtue makes you nice:
But when you do resist the pressing youth,
'Tis want of dear desire, to thaw the Virgin Ice.
And while your young adorers lye
All languishing and hopeless at your feet,
Raising new Trophies to your chastity,
Oh tell me, how you do remain discreet?
How you suppress the rising sighs,
And the soft yeilding soul that wishes in your Eyes?
While to th'admiring crow'd you nice are found;

Some dear, some secret, youth that gives the wound
Informs you, all your virtu's but a cheat
And Honour but a false disguise,
Your modesty a necessary bait
To gain the dull repute of being wise.

Deceive the foolish World deceive it on,
And veil your passions in your pride;
But now I've found your feebles by my own,
From me the needful fraud you cannot hide.
Tho tis a mighty power must move
The soul to this degree of love,
And tho with virtue I the World perplex,
Lysander finds the weakness of my sex,
So Helen while from Theseus arms she fled,
To charming Paris yeilds her heart and Bed.

To Amintas. Upon reading the Lives of some of the Romans,

Had'st thou, Amintas, liv'd in that great age,
When hardly Beauty was to nature known,
What numbers to thy side might'st thou engage
And conquer'd Kingdoms by thy looks alone?

That age when valor they did Beauty name,
When Men did justly our brave sex prefer,
'Cause they durst dye, and scorn the publick shame
Of adding Glory to the conqueror.

Had mighty Scipio had thy charming face,
Great Sophonisbe had refus'd to dye,
Her passion o're the sense of her disgrace
Had gain'd the more obliging victory.

Nor less wou'd Massanissa too have done
But to such Eyes, as to his Sword wou'd bow,
For neither sex can here thy fetters shun,
Being all Scipio, and Amintas too.

Had'st thou great Ctssar been, the greater Queen,
Wou'd trembling have her mortal Asps lay'd by,
In thee she had not only Ceesar seen,
But all she did adore in Antony.

Had daring Sextus had thy lovely shape,
The fairest Woman living had not dy'd
But blest the darkness that secur'd the Rape,
Suffering her Pleasure to have debauch't her Pride.

Nor had he stoln to Rome to have quencht his fire,
If thee resistless in his Camp he'd seen,
Thy Eyes had kept his virtue all intire,
And Rome a happy monarchy had been.

Had Pompey lookt like thee, tho he had prov'd
The vanquisht, yet from Egypts faithless King
He had received the vows of being belov'd,
In stead of Orders for his murdering.

But here, Amintas, thy misfortune lys,
Nor brave nor good are in our age esteem'd,
Content thee then with meaner victorys,
Unless that Glorious age cou'd be redeem'd.

On the first discovery of falseness in Amintas.

Make hast! make hast! my miserable soul,
To some unknown and solitary Grove,
Where nothing may thy Languishment controle
Where thou maist never hear the name of Love.
Where unconfin'd, and free, as whispering Air,
Thou maist caress and welcome thy despair:

Where no dissembl'd complisance may veil
The griefes with which, my soul, thou art opprest,
But dying, breath thyself out in a tale
That may declare the cause of thy unrest:
The toyles of Death 'twill render far more light
And soon convey thee to the shades of night.

Search then, my soul, some unfrequented place,
Some place that nature meant her own repose:
When she herself with-drew from human race,
Displeas'd with wanton Lovers vows and oaths.
Where Sol cou'd never dart a busy Ray,
And where the softer winds ne're met to play.

By the sad purling of some Rivulet
O're which the bending Yew and Willow grow,
That scarce the glimmerings of the day permit,
To view the melancholy Banks below,
Where dwells no noyse but what the murmurs make,
When the unwilling stream the shade forsakes.

There on a Bed of Moss and new-fain leaves,
Which the Triumphant Trees once proudly bore,
Tho now thrown off by every wind that breaths,
Despism by what they did adorn before,

And who, like useless me, regardless lye
While springing beautys do the boughs supply.

There lay thee down, my soul, and breath thy last,
And calmly to the unknown regions fly;
But e're thou dost thy stock of life exhaust,
Let the ungrateful know, why tis you dye.
Perhaps the gentle winds may chance to bear
Thy dying accents to Amintas ear.

Breath out thy Passion; tell him of his power
And how thy flame was once by thee approv'd.
How soon as wisht he was thy conqueror,
No sooner spoke of Love, but was belov'd.
His wonderous Eyes, what weak resistance found,
While every charming word begat a wound?

Here thou wilt grow impatient to be gone,
And thro my willing Eyes will silent pass,
Into the stream that gently glides along,
But stay thy hasty flight, (my Soul,) alas,
A thought more cruel will thy flight secure,
Thought, that can no admittance give to cure.
Think, how the prostrate Infidel now lys,
An humble suppliant at anothers feet,
Think, while he begs for pity from her Eyes.
He sacrifices thee with-out regreet.
Think, how the faithless treated thee last night,
And then, my tortur'd soul, assume thy flight.

To the fair Clarinda, who made Love to me, imagin'd more than Woman.

Fair lovely Maid, or if that Title be
Too weak, too Feminine for Nobler thee,
Permit a Name that more Approaches Truth:
And let me call thee, Lovely Charming Youth.
This last will justifie my soft complaint,
While that may serve to lessen my constraint;
And without Blushes I the Youth persue,
When so much beauteous Woman is in view.
Against thy Charms we struggle but in vain
With thy deluding Form thou giv'st us pain,
While the bright Nymph betrays us to the Swain.
In pity to our Sex sure thou wer't sent,
That we might Love, and yet be Innocent:
For sure no Crime with thee we can commit;
Or if we shou'd thy Form excuses it.
For who, that gathers fairest Flowers believes
A Snake lies hid beneath the Fragrant Leaves.

Thou beauteous Wonder of a different kind,
Soft Claris with the dear d lexis join'd;
When e'r the Manly part of thee, wou'd plead
Thou tempts us with the Image of the Maid,
While we the noblest Passions do extend
The Love to Hermes, Aphrodite the Friend.

WESTMINSTER DROLLERY, 1671.

A SONG.

That Beauty I ador'd before,
I now as much despise:
'Tis Money only makes the Whore:
She that for love with her Crony lies,
Is chaste: But that's the Whore that kisses for prize.

Let Jove with Gold his Danac woo,
It shall be no rule for me:
Nay, 't may be I may do so too,
When I'me as old as he.
Till then Pie never hire the thing that's free.

If Coin must your affection Imp,
Pray get some other Friend:
My Pocket ne're shall be my Pimp,
I never that intend,
Yet can be noble too^ if I see they mend.

Since Loving was a Liberal Art,
How canst thou trade for gain?
The pleasure is on your part,
'Tis we Men take the pain:
And being so, must Women have the gain?

No, no, Tie never farm your Bed,
Nor your Smock-Tenant be:
I hate to rent your white and red,
You shall not let your Love to me:
I court a Mistris, not a Landlady.

A Pox take him that first set up,
Th' Excise of Flesh and Skin:
And since it will no better be,
Let's both to kiss begin;
To kiss freely: if not , you may go spin.

MISCELLANY, 1685.

To SIR WILLIAM CLIFTON

Sir,

I am very sensible how the ill-natur'd World has been pleased to Judge of almost all Dedications, and when not addrest to themselves will not let 'em pass without the imputation of Flattery; for there is scarce any Man so just to allow those Praises to another in which he does not immediately share in some degree himself, nor can the Fantastic Humors of the Age agree in point of Merit, but every Mans Vertue is measured according to the sence another has of it, and not by its own intrinsic value, so that if another does not see with my Eyes and judge with my Sence, I must be Branded with the Crime of Fools and Cowards: nor will they be undeceived in an Error that so agree ably flatters them, either by a better knowledge of the Person commended, or by a right understanding from any other Judgment; they hate to be convinced of what will make no part of their satisfaction when they are so, for as 'tis natural to despise all those that have no vertue at all, so 'tis as natural to Envy those we find have more than our selves instead of imitating 'em: and I have heard a Man rail at a Dedication for being all over Flattery, and Damn it in gross, who when it has been laid before him, and he has been asked to answer according to his Conscience, and upon Honour to every particular, could not contradict one single Vertue that has been justly given there, yet angry at being convinced has cry'd, with a peevish, uneasie tone.— YET I DON'T KNOW HOW, NOR I DON'T KNOW WHAT BUT 'TIS ALL TOGETHER METHINKS A PIECE OF FLATTERY When indeed the business was, be did not know how to afford him so good a Character, nor be did not know what other reason he had to find fault with it, and was only now afflicted to find 'twas all true; whereas before he charged it all on the effects of some little sinister end or advantage of the Author.

'Tis therefore, Sir, that I have taken the Liberty here of addressing my self to one, whose Generosity and Goodness has prevented any such Scandal, and secured me from the imputation of Flattery by rendring this, but a small part of that Duty only, which I have so long owed you; 'tis only, Sir, my debt of gratitude I pay, or rather an humble acknowledgment of what I ought to pay you; for favours of that nature are not easily returned, and one must be a great while discharging it out of the Barren Stock of Poetry; but where my own failed, I borrowed of my Friends, who were all ready to give me Credit for so good and just an occasion, and we all soon agreed where first we should begin the work of gratitude. For, Sir, your worth is every where known, and valued; it bears the Royal stamp and passes for currant to every ready hand; Loyalty being that standard Vertue of the Soul which finds its price all over the World; nor is it in these our glorious days, who bears that Rate now, but who has always done so through Fate and Fortune; dyed in the true Grain, not to be varied with every glittering Sun-shine, nor lost in every falling Shower, but stanch to its first beautiful colour, indures all weather.

Nor is it enough that where you are known, you are beloved and blest but you, whose Quality and Fortune elevate you above the common Crow ought to have your Loyal Names fixed every where, as great and leading Examples to the rest, as the Genius of your Country and the Star that influences, where your Lustre shines. You, who in spight of all the Follies import from France so much in fashion here, still retain, and still maintain the good old English Customs of Noble Hospitality, and treat the under world about you, even into good nature and Loyalty; and have kept your Country honest, while else- where for want of such great Patrons and Presidents, Faction and Sedition have over-run those Villages where Ignorance abounde and got footing almost every where, whose Inhabitants are a sort of Bruit that ought no more to be left to themselves than Fire, and are as Mischievo and as Destructive. While every great Landlord is a kind of Monarch that awes and civilizes 'em into Duty and Allegiance, and whom because they know, they Worship with a Reverence equal to what they would pay their King, whose Representative they take him at least to be if not that of himself, since they know no greater or more indulgent; and are sure to of his opinion, he's their Oracle, their very Gospel, and whom they'll soon credit; never was new Religion, Misunderstanding, and Rebellion known in Countries till Gentlemen of ancient Families reformed their way of living to the new Mode, pulled down their great Halls, retrenched their Servants, and confined themselves to scanty lodgings in the City, starved the Poor of their Parish, and rackt their Tenants to keep the Taudry Jilt in Town a hundred times more expensive, but you, Sir, retain still the perfect measure of true Honour, you understand the joys and comforts of life and blest retreat; you value Courts tho you do not always shine there, you dare be brave, liberal, and honest tho you do not always behold the Illustrious Pattern of all Glorious Vertue in your King, and absent from the lavish City. You are pleased and contented with the favour of your Monarch, tho you have no need of his Bounty, dare serve him with your Life and Fortune, and can find your reward in your own Vertue and Merit; this I dare avow to all the World is your Character in short, for which your lasting Name shall live, when the turbulent, busie hot-brain'd disturbers of their own tranquillity and the Kingdoms Peace, shall live in fear, die in Shame and their memory rot in the forgotten Grave, or stand to after Ages Branded and Reproached, while we can never enough Celebrate that Glorious one of yours; nor knew we where to fix it to render it Durable to all Eternity so well as to lasting Verse, that out-wears Time and Marble. If anything within can contribute to the diversion of your Hours of least concern, 'twill be sufficient recompence to all who beg your Patronage here, especially

Sir,
Your obliged
and most humble Servant,
A. BEHN.

MISCELLANY, 1685.

On the Death of the late Earl of Rochester

Mourn, Mourn, ye Muses, all your loss deplore,
The Young, the Noble Strephon is no more.
Yes, yes, he fled quick as departing Light,
And ne're shall rise from Deaths eternal Night,
So rich a Prize the Stygian Gods ne're bore,
Such Wit, such Beauty, never grac'd their Shore.
He was but lent this duller World t' improve
In all the charms of Poetry, and Love;
Both were his gift, which freely he bestow'd,
And like a God, dealt to the wond'ring Crowd.
Scorning the little Vanity of Fame,
Spight of himself attained a Glorious name.
But oh! in vain was all his peevish Pride,
The Sun as soon might his vast Lustre hide,
As piercing, pointed, and more lasting bright,
As suffering no vicissitudes of Night.
Mourn, Mourn, ye Muses, all your loss deplore,
The Young, the Noble Strephon is no more.

Now uninspir'd upon your Banks we lye,
Unless when we wou'd mourn his Elegie;
His name's a Genius that wou'd Wit dispense,
And give the Theme a Soul, the Words a Sense.
But all fine thought that Ravisht when it spoke,
With the soft Youth eternal leave has took;
Uncommon Wit that did the soul o'recome,
Is buried all in Strephorn's Worship'd Tomb;
Satyr has lost its Art, its Sting is gone,
The Fop and Cully now may be undone;
That dear instructing Rage is now allay'd,
And no sharp Pen dares tell 'em how they've stray'd;
Bold as a God was ev'ry lash he took,
But kind and gentle the chastising stroke.

Mourn, Mourn, ye Youths, whom Fortune has betray'd,
The last Reproacher of your Vice is dead.
Mourn, all ye Beauties, put your Cyprus on,
The truest Swain that e're Ador'd you's gone;
Think how he lov'd, and writ, and sigh'd, and spoke,
Recall his Meen, his Fashion, and his Look.
By what dear Arts the Soul he did surprize,
Soft as his Voice, and charming as his Eyes.
Bring Garlands all of never-dying Flow'rs,
Bedew'd with everlasting falling Show'rs;
Fix your fair eyes upon your victim'd Slave,
Sent Gay and Young to his untimely Grave.
See where the Noble Swain Extended lies,
Too sad a Triumph of your Victories;
Adorn'd with all the Graces Heav'n e're lent,
All that was Great, Soft, Lovely, Excellent
You've laid into his early Monument.
Mourn, Mourn, ye Beauties, your sad loss deplore,
The Young, the Charming Strephon is no more.

Mourn, all ye little Gods of Love, whose Darts
Have lost their wonted power of piercing hearts;
Lay by the gilded Quiver and the Bow,
The useless Toys can do no Mischief now,
Those Eyes that all your Arrows points inspir'd,
Those Lights that gave ye fire are now retir'd,
Cold as his Tomb, pale as your Mothers Doves;
Bewail him then oh all ye little Loves,
For you the humblest Votary have lost
That ever your Divinities could boast;
Upon your hands your weeping Heads decline,
And let your wings encompass round his Shrine;
In stead of Flow'rs your broken Arrows strow,
And at his feet lay the neglected Bow.
Mourn, all ye little Gods, your loss deplore,
The soft, the Charming Strephon is no more.

Large was his Fame, but short his Glorious Race,
Like young Lucretius liv'd and dy'd apace.
So early Roses fade, so over all
They cast their fragrant scents, then softly fall,
While all the scatter'd perfum'd leaves declare,
How lovely 'twas when whole, how sweet, how fair.
Had he been to the Roman Empire known,
When great Augustus fill'd the peaceful Throne;
Had he the noble wond'rous Poet seen,
And known his Genius, and survey'd his Meen,
(When Wits, and Heroes grac'd Divine abodes,)
He had increased the number of their Gods;
The Royal Judge had Temples rear'd to's name.
And made him as Immortal as his Fame;
In Love and Verse his Ovid he'ad out-done,
And all his Laurels, and his Julia won.
Mourn, Mourn, unhappy World, his loss deplore,
The great, the charming Strepbon is no more.

SONG By A. B.

Cease, cease, Aminta, to complain,
Thy Languishment give o're,
Why shoud'st thou sigh because the Swain
Another does Adore?
Those Charms, fond Maid, that vanquish'd thee,
Have many a Conquest won,
And sure he could not cruel be,
And leave 'em all undon.

The Youth a Noble temper bears,
Soft and compassionate,
And thou canst only blame thy Stars,
That made thee love too late;
Yet had their Influence all been kind
They had not cross'd my Fate,
The tend'rest hours must have an end,
And Passion has its date.

The softest love grows cold and shy,
The face so late ador'd,
Now unregarded passes by,
Or grows at last abhor'd;
All things in Nature fickle prove,
See how they glide away;
Think so in time thy hopeless love
Will die, as Flowers decay.

While, Iris, I at distance gaze,
And feed my greedy eyes,
That wounded heart, that dyes for you,
Dull gazing can't suffice;
Hope is the Food of Love-sick minds,
On that alone 'twill Feast,
The nobler part which Loves refines,
No other can digest.

In vain, too nice and Charming Maid,
I did suppress my Cares;
In vain my rising sighs I stay'd,
And stop'd my falling tears;
The Flood would swell, the Tempest rise,
As my despair came on;
When from her Lovely cruel Eyes,
I found I was undone.
Yet at your feet while thus I lye,
And languish by your Eyes,
'Tis far more glorious here to dye,
Than gain another Prize.
Here let me sigh, here let me gaze,
And wish at least to find
As raptur'd nights, and tender days,
As he to whom you're kind.

OUR FATHER,

O Wondrous condescention of a God!
To poor unworthy sinful flesh and blood;
Lest the high Mistery of Divinity,
Thy sacred Title, shou'd too Awful be;
Lest trembling prostrates should not freely come,
As to their Parent, to their native home;
Lest Thy incomprehensible God-head shou'd
Not by dull Man; be rightly understood;
Thou deignst to take a name, that fits our sense,
Yet lessens not Thy glorious Excellence.

WHICH ART IN HEAVEN,

Thy Mercy ended not, when thou didst own
Poor lost and out-cast Man to be thy Son;

'Twas not enough the Father to dispense,
In Heaven thou gav'st us an Inheritance;
A Province, where thou'st deign'd each Child a share;
Advance, my tim'rous Soul, thou needst not fear,
Thou hast a God! a God and Father! there.

HALLOWED BE THY NAME,

For ever be it, may my Pious Verse,
That shall thy great and glorious name rehearse,
By singing Angels still repeated be,
And tune a Song that may be worthy thee;
While all the Earth with Ecchoing Heav'n shall joyn,
To Magnifie a Being so Divine.

THY KINGDOM COME,

Prepare, my Soul, 'gainst that Triumphant day,
Adorn thy self with all that's Heavenly gay,
Put on the Garment, which no spot can stain,
And with thy God! thy King! and Father! Reign;
When all the Joyful Court of Heaven shall be
One everlasting day of Jubilee;
Make my Soul fit but there to find a room,
Then when thou wilt, Lord let thy Kingdom come.

THY WILL BE DONE

With all submission prostrate I resign
My Soul, my Faculties, and Will to thine;
For thou, Oh Lord, art Holy, Wise, and Just,
And raising Man from forth the common dust,
Hast set thy Sacred Image on his Soul,
And shall the Pot the Potters hand controul?
Poor boasting feeble Clay, that Error shun,
Submit and let th' Almighty's Will be done.

IN EARTH AS IT IS IN HEAVEN.

For there the Angels, and the Saints rejoyce,
Resigning all to the blest Heavenly Voice;
Behold the Seraphins his Will obey,
Wilt thou less humble be, fond Man, than they?
Behold the Cherubins and Pow'rs Divine,

And all the Heavenly Host in Homage joyn;
Shall their Submission yield, and shall not thine?
Nay, shall even God submit to Flesh and Blood?
For our Redemption, our Eternal good,
Shall he submit to stripes, nay even to die

A Death reproachful, and of Infamy?
Shall God himself submit, and shall not I?

Vain, stubborn Fool, draw not thy ruine on,
But as in Heav'n; on Earth God's Will be done;

GIVE US THIS DAY OUR DAILY BREAD,

For oh my God! as boasting as we are,
We cannot live without thy heavenly care,
With all our Pride, not one poor Morsel's gain'd,
Till by thy wondrous Bounty first obtained;
With all our flatter'd Wit, our fanci'd sense,
We have not to one Mercy a pretence
Without the aid of thy Omnipotence.

Oh God, so fit my soul, that I may prove
A pitied Object of thy Grace and Love;
May my soul be with Heavenly Manna fed,
And deign my grosser part thy daily bread.

AND FORGIVE US OUR TRESPASSES

How prone we are to Sin, how sweet were made
The pleasures, our resistless hearts invade!
Of all my Crimes, the breach of all thy Laws
Love, soft bewitching Love! has been the cause;
Of all the Paths that Vanity has trod,
That sure will soonest be forgiven of God;
If things on Earth may be to Heaven resembled,
It must be love, pure, constant, undissembled:
But if to Sin by chance the Charmer press,
Forgive, O Lord, forgive our Trespasses.

AS WE FORGIVE THEM THAT TRESPASS AGAINST US,

Oh that this grateful, little Charity,
Forgiving others all their sins to me,
May with my God for mine attoning be.
I've sought around, and found no foe in view,
Whom with the least Revenge I would pursue,
My God, my God, dispense thy Mercies too.

LEAD US NOT INTO TEMPTATION

Thou but permits it, Lord, 'tis we go on,
And give our selves the Provocation;
'Tis we, that prone to pleasures which invite.
Seek all the Arts to heighten vain delight;
But if without some Sin we cannot move,
May mine proceed no higher than to love;

And may thy vengeance be the less severe,
Since thou hast made the object lov'd so fair.

BUT DELIVER US FROM EVIL.

From all the hasty Fury Passion breeds,
And into deaf and blinded Error leads,
From words that bear Damnation in the sound,
And do the Soul as well as Honour wound,
That by degrees of Madness lead us on
To Indiscretion, Shame, Confusion;
From Fondness, Lying, and Hypocrisie,
From my neglect of what I ow to thee;
From Scandal, and from Pride, divert my thought,
And from my Neighbour grant I covet nought;
From black Ingratitude, and Treason, Lord,
Guard me, even in the least unreverend word.
In my Opinion, grant, O Lord, I may, \
Be guided in the true and rightful way,
And he that guides me may not go astray; J
Do thou, oh Lord, instruct me how to know
Not whither, but which way I am to go;
For how should I an unknown passage find,
When my instructing Guide himself is blind.
All Honour, Glory, and all Praise be given
To Kings on Earth, and to our God in Heaven.

Amen.

SELINDA and CLORIS, made in an Entertainment at Court. By Mrs. A. B.

Selinda
As young Selinda led her Flock,
Beneath the Shelter of a shaded Rock,
The Melancholy Cloris by,
Thus to the Lovely Maid did sighing cry.

Cloris
Selinda, you too lightly prize,
The powerful Glorys of your Eyes;
To suffer young Alexis to adore,
Alexis, whom Love made my slave before;
I first adorn'd him with my Chains,
He Sigh'd beneath the rigour of my Reign
And can that Conquest now be worth your
A Votary you deserve who ne'er knew how,
To any Altars but your own to bow.

Selinda

Is it your Friendship or your Jealousie,
That brings this timely aid to me?
With Reason we that Empire quit,
Who so much Rigour shows,
And 'twould declare more Love than Wit,
Not to recall his Vows.
If Beauty could Alexis move,
He might as well be mine;
He saw the Errors of his Love,
He saw how long in vain he strove,
And did your scorn decline;
And, Cloris, I the Gods may imitate,
And humble Penitents receive, tho late.

Cloris
Mistaken Maid, can his Devotion prove
Agreeable or true,
Who only offers broken Vows of Love?
Vows which, Belinda, are my due.
How often prostrate at my feet h'as lain,
Imploring Pity for his Pain?
My heart a thousand ways he strove to win,
Before it let the Charming Conqueror in;
Ah then how soon the Amorous heat was laid!
How soon he broke the Vows he made!
Slighting the Trophies he had won.
And smiling saw me sigh for being undone.

Selinda
Enough, enough, my dear abandon'd Maid,
Enough thy Eyes, thy Sighs, thy Tongue have said,
In all the Groves, on all the Plains,
'Mongst all the Shepherds, all the Swains,
I never saw the Charms cou'd move
My yet unconquer'd heart, to Love;
And tho a God Alexis were,
He should not Rule the Empire here.

Cloris
Then from his charming Language fly;
Or thou'rt undone as well as I;
The God of Love is sure his Friend,
Who taught him all his Arts,
And when a Conquest he designed,
He furnish'd him with Darts;
His Quiver, and his gilded Bow,
To his assistance brings,
And having given the fatal Blow,
Lends him his fleeting wings.
Tho not a Cottage-Slave, can be,
Before the Conquest, so submiss as he,

To Fold your sheep, to gather Flowers,
To Pipe and sing, and sigh away your hours;
Early your Flocks to fragrant Meads,
Or cooling shades, and Springs he Leads;
Weaves Garlands, or go seek your Lambs,
That struggle from their bleating Dams,
Or any humble bus'ness do,
But once a Victor, he's a Tyrant too.

Belinda
Cloris, such little Services would prove
Too mean, to be repaid with Love;
A Look, a Nod, a Smile would quit that score,
And she deserves to be undone, that pays a Shepherd more,

Cloris
His new-blown Passion if Selinda Scorn,
Alexis may again to me return.

Selinda
Secure thy Fears, the Vows he makes to me
I send a Present, back to thee;

Cloris
Then we will sing, in every Grove,
The greatness of your Mind,

Selinda
. . . And I your Love.

Both
And all the Day,
With Pride and Joy,
We'll let the Neighboring Shepherds see,
That none like us,
Did e'er express,
The heights of Love and Amity;
And all the day, &c.

A PINDARIC to Mr. P. who sings finely.

Damon, altho you waste in vain
That pretious breath of thine,
Where lies a Pow'r in every strain,
To take in any other heart, but mine;
Yet do not cease to sing, that I may know,
By what soft Charms and Arts,
What more than Humane 'tis you do,
To take, and keep your hearts;

Or have you Vow'd never to wast your breath,
But when some Maid must fall a Sacrifice,
As Indian Priests prepare a death,
For Slaves t'addorn their Victories,
Your Charm's as powerful, if I live,
For I as sensible shall be,
What wound you can, to all that hear you, give,
As if you wounded me;
And shall as much adore your wondrous skill,
As if my heart each dying Note cou'd kill.

And yet I should not tempt my Fate,
Nor trust my feeble strength,
Which does with ev'ry softning Note abate
And may at length
Reduce me to the wretched Slave I hate;
Tis strange extremity in me,
To venture on a doubtful Victory,
Where if you fail, I gain no more,
Than what I had before;
But 'twill certain comfort bring,

If I unconquer'd do escape from you;
If I can live, and hear you sing,
No other Forces can my Soul subdue;
Sing, Damon^ then, and let each Shade,
Which with thy Heavenly voice is happy made,
Bear witness if my courage be not great,
To hear thee sing, and make a safe retreat.

On the Author of that Excellent Book Intituled The Way to Health, Long Life, and Happiness

Hail, Learned Bard! who dost thy power dispence,
And show'st us the first State of Innocence
In that blest golden Age, when Man was young,
When the whole Race was Vigorous and strong;
When Nature did her wond'rous dictates give,
And taught the Noble Savage how to live;
When Christal Streams, and every plenteous Wood
Afforded harmless drink, and wholsom food;
E'er that ingratitude in Man was found,
His Mother Earth with Iron Ploughs to wound;
When unconfin'd, the spacious Plains produced
What Nature crav'd, and more than Nature us'd;
When every Sense to innocent delight
Th' agreeing Elements unforc'd invite;
When Earth was gay, and Heaven was kind and bright,
And nothing horrid did perplex the sight;
Unprun'd the Roses and the Jes'min grew,

Nature each day drest all the World anew,
And Sweets without Mans aid each Moment grew;
Till wild Debauchery did Mens minds invade,
And Vice, and Luxury became a Trade;
Surer than War it laid whole Countrys wast,
Not Plague nor Famine ruins half so fast;
By swift degrees we took that Poison in,
Regarding not the danger, nor the sin;
Delightful, Gay, and Charming was the Bait,
While Death did on th' inviting Pleasure wait,
And ev'ry Age produc'd a feebler Race,
Sickly their days, and those declined apace,
Scarce Blossoms Blow, and Wither in less space.
Till Nature thus declining by degrees,
We have recourse to rich restoratives,
By dull advice from some of Learned Note,
We take the Poison for the Antidote;
Till sinking Nature cloy'd with full supplys,
O'er-charg'd grows fainter, Languishes and dies.

These are the Plagues that o'er this Island reign,
And have so many threescore thousands slain;
Till you the saving Angel, whose blest hand
Have sheath'd that Sword, that threatned half the Land;
More than a Parent, Sir, we you must own,
They give but life, but you prolong it on;
You even an equal power with Heav'n do shew,
Give us long life, and lasting Vertue too:
Such were the mighty Patriarchs, of old,
Who God in all his Glory did behold,
Inspir'd like you, they Heavens Instructions show'd,
And were as Gods amidst the wandring Croud;
Not he that bore th' Almighty Wand cou'd give
Diviner Dictates, how to eat, and live.
And so essential was this cleanly Food,
For Mans eternal health, eternal good,
That God did for his first-lov'd Race provide,
What thou by Gods example hast prescrib'd:
O mai'st thou live to justifie thy fame,
To Ages lasting as thy glorious Name!
May thy own life make thy vast Reasons good,
(Philosophy admir'd and understood,)
To every sense 'tis plain, 'tis great, and clear,
And Divine Wisdom does o'er all appear;
Learning and Knowledge do support the whole,
And nothing can the mighty truth controul;
Let Fools and Mad-men thy great work condemn,
I've tri'd thy Method, and adore thy Theme;
Adore the Soul that cou'd such truths discern,
And scorn the fools that want the sense to learn.

This Little, Silent, Gloomy Monument,
Contains all that was sweet and innocent;
The softest pratler that e'er found a Tongue,
His Voice was Musick and his Words a Song;
Which now each List'ning Angel smiling hears,
Such pretty Harmonies compose the Spheres;
Wanton as unfledg'd Cupids, ere their Charms
Had learn'd the little arts of doing harms;
Fair as young Cherubins, as soft and kind,
And tho translated could not be refin'd;
The Seventh dear pledge the Nuptial Joys had given,
Toil'd here on Earth, retir'd to rest in Heaven;
Where they the shining Host of Angels fill,
Spread their gay wings before the Throne, and smile.

And how, and how, Mesieurs! what do you say
To our good Moderate, Conscientious Play?
Not Whig, nor Tory, here can take Offence;
It Libels neither Patriot, Peer, nor Prince,
Nor Shrieve, nor Burgess, nor the Reverend Gown.
Faith here's no Scandal worth eight hundred pound;
Your Damage is at most but half-a-Crown.
Only this difference you must allow,
'Tis you receive th' Affront and pay us too,
Wou'd Rebell WARD had manag'd matters so.
Here's no Reflections on Damn'd Witnesses,
We scorn such out-of-Fash'on'd Things as These;
They fail to be believ'd, and fail to please.
No Salamanca Doctor-ship abus'd,
Not a Malicious States-man here accus'd;
No Smutty Scenes, no intrigues up Stairs,
That make your City Wives in Love with Players.
But here are fools of every sort and Fashion,
Except State-Fools, the Tools of Reformation,
Or Cullys of the Court Association.
And those Originals decline so fast
We shall have none to Copy by at last;
Here's Jo, and Jack a pair of whining Fools,
And Leigh and I brisk Lavish keeping Fools,
He's for Mischief all, and carry's it on
With Fawne and Sneere as Jilting Whigg has done.
And like theirs too his Projects are o'rethrown.

THIRSIS and AMARILLIS.

Thirsis
Why, Amarilis dost thou walk alone,
And the gay pleasures of the Meadows shun?
Why to the silent Groves dost thou retire,
When uncompell'd by the Suns scorching fire?
Musing with folded Arms, and down-cast look,
Or pensive yield to thy supporting Hook:
Is Damon false? and has his Vows betray'd,
And born the Trophies to some other Maid?

Amarillis
The Gods forbid I should survive to see
The fatal day he were unjust to me.
Nor is my Courage, or my Love so poor

T' out-live that Scorn'd, and miserable hour;
Rather let Solves my new-yean'd Lambs devour,
Wither ye Verdant Grass, dry up ye Streams,
And let all Nature turn to vast extreams:
In Summer let the Boughs be cale and dry,

And now gay Flowers the wandring Spring supply,
But with my Damons Love, Let all that's charming die.

Thirsis
Why then this dull retreat, if he be true,
Or, Amarillis, is the change in you?
You love some Swains more rich in Herds and Flocks,
For none can be more powerful in his looks;
His shape, his meen, his hair, his wondrous face,
And on the Plaines, none dances with his Grace;
'Tis true, in Piping he does less excell.

Amarillis
The Musick of his Voice can Charm as well,
When tun'd to words of Love, and sighs among,
With the soft tremblings of his bashful tongue,
And, Thirsts, you accuse my Faith in vain,
To think it wavering, for another Swain;
Tis admiration now that fills my soul,
And does ev'n love suspend, if not controul.
My thoughts are solemn all, and do appear
With wonder in my Eyes, and not despair!
My heart is entertain'd with silent Joys,

And I am pleas'd above the Mirth of Noise.

Thirsis
What new-born pleasure can divert you so?
Pray let me hear, that I may wonder too.

Amarillis
Last night, by yonder purling stream I stood,
Pleas'd with the murmurs of the little Flood,
Who in its rapid glidings bore away
The Fringing Flow'rs, that made the Bank so gay,
Which I compared to fickle Swains, who invade
First this, then that deceiv'd, and yielding Maid:
Whose flattering Vows an easie passage find,
Then unregarded leave 'em far behind,
To sigh their Ruin to the flying Wind.
So the soild flow'rs their rifled Beauties hung,
While the triumphant Ravisher passes on.
This while I sighing view'd, I heard a voice
That made the Woods, the Groves, and Hills rejoyce.
Who eccho'd back the charming sound again,
Answering the Musick of each softning strain,
And told the wonder over all the Plain.
Young Silvio 'twas that tun'd his happy Pipe,
The best that ever grac'd a Shepherds Lip!
Silvio of Noble Race, yet not disdains
To mix his harmony with Rustic Swains,
To th' humble Shades th' Illustrious Youth resorts,
Shunning the false delights of gaudy Courts,
For the more solid happiness of Rural sports.
Courts which his Noble Father long pursu'd,
And Serv'd till he out-serv'd their gratitude.

Thirsis
Oh Amarillis, let that tale no more
Remembred be on the Arcadian Shore,
Lest Mirth should on our Meads no more be found,
But Stafford's Story should throughout resound,
And fill with pitying cryes the Echoes all around.

Amarillis
Arcadia, keep your peace, but give me leave,
Who knew the Heroes Loyalty^ to grieve;
Once, Tbirsis, by th' Arcadian Kings Commands,
I left these Shades, to visit forein Lands;
Imploy'd in public toils of State Affairs,
Unusual with my Sex, or to my Years;
There 'twas my chance, so Fortune did ordain,
To see this great, this good, this God-like Man:
Brave, Pious, Loyal, Just, without constraint,
The Soul all Angell, and the Man a Saint;

His temper'd mind no Passion e'er inflam'd,
But when his King and Countrey were profan'd;
Then oft I've seen his generous blood o'er spread
His awful face, with a resenting Red,
In Anger quit the Room, and would disdain
To herd with the Rebellious Publican.
But, Thirsts, 'twould a worship'd Volume fill,
If I the Heroes wondrous Life should tell;
His Vertues were his Crime, like God he bow'd
A necessary Victim to the frantick Croud;
So a tall sheltring Oak that long had stood,
The mid-days shade, and glory of the Wood;
Whose aged boughs a reverence did command,
Fell lop'd at last by an Ignoble hand:
And all his branches are in pieces torn,
That Victors grac'd, and did the Wood adorn.
With him young Silvio, who compos'd his Joys,
The darling of his Soul and of his Eyes,
Inheriting the Vertues of his Sire,
But all his own is his Poetic fire;
When young, the Gods of Love, and Wit did grace
The pointed, promised Beautys of his face,
Which ripening years did to perfection bring,
And taught him how to Love, and how to Sing.

Thirsis
But what, dear Amarillis, was the Theam
The Noble Silvio Sung by yonder Stream?

Amarillis
Not of the Shepherds, nor their Rural Loves.
The Song was Glorious tho 'twas sung in Groves!
Camilla s Death the skilful Youth inspir'd,
As if th' Heroic Maid his Soul had fir'd;
Such life was in his Song, such heat, such flight,
As he had seen the Royal Virgin fight.
He made her deal her wounds with Graceful Art,
With vigorous Air fling the unfailing Dart,
And form'd her Courage to his own great heart.
Never was fighting in our Sex a Charm,
Till Silvio did the bright Camilla Arm;
With Noble Modesty he shews us how
To be at once Hero and Woman too.
Oh Conquering Maid! how much thy Fame has won,
In the Arcadian Language to be sung,
And by a Swain so soft, so sweet, so young.

Thirsis
Well hast thou spoke the noble Silvio's Praise,
For I have often heard his charming lays;
Oft has he blest the Shades with strains Divine,

Took many a Virgins heart, and Ravish'd mine.
Long may he sing in every Field and Grove,
And teach the Swains to Pipe, the Maids to Love.

Amarillis

Daphnis, and Colin Pipe not half so well,
E'en Dions mighty self he does excell;
As the last Lover of the Muses, blest,
The last and young in Love are always best;
And She her darling Lover does requite
With all the softest Arts of Noblest Wit.

Thirsis

Oh may he dedicate his Youth to her!
Thus let 'em live, and love upon the square,
But see Alexis homeward leads his Flock,
And brouzing Goats descend from yonder Rock;
The Sun is hasting on to Thetis Bed,
See his faint Beams have streak'd the Sky with Red.
Let's home e'er night approach, and all the way
You shall of Silvio sing, while I will play.

GILDON'S MISCELLANY, 1692.

VENUS and CUPID.

Venus

Cupid, my darling Cupid, and my Joy,
Thy Mother Venus calls, come away, come away.

Cupid

Alas! I cannot, I am at Play.

Venus

Fond Boy, I do command thee, haste;
Thy precious Hours no longer waste:
In Groves and Cottages you make abode,
Too mean a Condescention for a God!
On barren Mountains idly play,
For shame thou Wanton, come away, come away!

All useless lies thy Bow and Darts,
That should be wounding heedless Hearts:
The Swain that guards his Dove,
Alas! no Leisure has for Love:
His Flocks and Heards are all his Joy,
Then leave the Shades and come away, come away,

Cupid

Alas! what would you have me do?
Command and I'll Obedience shew.

Venus
Hye then to Cities and to Court,
Where all the Young and Fair resort;
There try thy Power, let fly thy Darts,
And bring me in some noble Hearts,
Worthy to be by thee undone,
For here's no Glory to be won.

Cupid
Mistaken Queen, look down and see,
What Trophies are prepared for thee,
What glorious Slaves are destin'd me.

Venus
Now, by my self, a Noble Throng;
How Fair the Nymphs, the Swains how Young!
No wonder if my little Loves
Delight and play in Shades and Groves.

Cupid
Then, Mother, here I'll bend my Bow,
And bring you wounded Hearts enough.

Venus
My pretty Charming Wanton, do.

Chorus
'Tis thus we over Mortals reign,
And thus we Adoration gain
From the proud Monarch to the humble Swain.

Verses design d by Mrs. A. Behn to be sent to a fair Lady, that desired she would absent herself
to cure her Love. Left unfinished.

In vain to Woods and Deserts I retire,
To shun the lovely Charmer I admire,
Where the soft Breezes do but fann my Fire!
In vain in Grotto's dark unseen I lie,
Love pierces where the Sun could never spy.
No place, no Art his Godhead can exclude,
The Dear Distemper reigns in Solitude:
Distance, alas, contributes to my Grief;
No more, of what fond Lovers call, Relief
Than to the wounded Hind does sudden Flight
From the chast Goddesses pursuing Sight:
When in the Heart the fatal Shaft remains,

And darts the Venom through our bleeding Veins.
If I resolve no longer to submit
My self a wretched Conquest to your Wit,
More swift than fleeting Shades, ten thousand Charms
From your bright Eyes that Rebel Thought disarms:
The more I strugl'd, to my Grief I found
My self in Cupid's Chains more surely bound:
Like Birds in Nets, the more I strive, I find
My self the faster in the Snare confin'd.

Verses by Madam Behn, never before printed. On a Conventicle.

Behold that Race, whence England's Woes proceed,
The Viper's Nest, where 'all our Mischiefs breed,
There, guided, by Inspiration, Treason speaks,
And through the Holy Bag-pipe Legion squeaks.
The Nation's Curse, Religion's ridicule,
The Rabble's God, the Politicians Tool,
Scorn of the Wise, and Scandal of the Just,
The Villain's Refuge, and the Women's Lust.

GILDON'S CHORUS POETARUM, 1694.

By Madam Behn.

I.
The Gods are not more blest than he,
Who fixing his glad eyes on thee,
With thy bright Rays his senses chears,
And drinks with ever thirsty Ears,
The charming Musick of thy Tongue
Does ever hear and ever long,
That sees with more than humane Grace
Sweet smiles adorn thy Angel Face.

II.
So when with kinder Beams you shine,
And so appear much more Divine,
My feebled Sense and dazzled Sight \
No more support the glorious Light,
And the fierce torrent of Delight. J
O then I feel my Life decay,
My ravish'd Soul then flies away;
Then Faintness does my Limbs surprize,
And Darkness swims before my Eyes.

III.

Then my Tongue fails, and from my Brow
The Liquid Drops in Silence flow;
Then wand'ring Fires run thro my Blood,
Then Cold binds up the languid Flood;
All Pale and Breathless then I lie,
I sigh, I tremble, and I die.

MUSES MERCURY, June, 1707.

The Complaint of the poor Cavaliers.

I.

Give me the Man that's hollow
Since he is the only Fellow,
For Honesty's out of Date;
And he's the only Gallant
That shew'd himself so Valiant,
To cut off his Master's Pate.
These these be the Men that flaunt,
As if they were Sons of Gaunt,
And ev'ry Knave
Is Fine and Brave,
While the poor Cavalier's in want.

II.

The Man that chang'd his Note,
And he who has turn'd his Coat,
Shall now have a good Reward;
He's either made a Knight,
Or else by this good Light,
A very Reverend Lord:
And let him be so for me,
I'm as gay and as good as he.

III.

Hang Sorrow, why should we repine,
We'll drive down our Grief with good Wine,
Not caring for those that rise;
For had they been but true Men,
They never had been new Men,

And we had ne'er been wise.
The Blockhead that merits most,
That has all his Fortune lost,
Must now be turn'd out
And a new-found Rout,
Of Courtiers rule the Roast.

The next Verses are so tender, that one may see the Author writ 'em with no affected Passion. And indeed she had no need to affect what was so natural to her.

On a Pin that hurt Amintas' Eye.

Injurious, how durst thou steal so nigh?
To touch, nay worse, to hurt his precious Eye.
Base Instrument, so ill thou'st play'd thy part,
Wounding his Eye, thou'st wounded my poor Heart,
And for each pity'd Drop his Eye did shed,
My sympathizing Heart a thousand bled:
Too daring Pin, was there no Tincture good,
To bath thy Point, but my Amintas' Blood?

Cou'd thy Ambition teach thee so to sin?
Was that a Place for thee to revel in?
'Twas there thy Mistress had design'd to be,
And must she find a Rival too in thee?
Curs'd Fate! that I shou'd harbour thee so long,
And thou at last conspire to do me wrong:
Tho well I knew thy Nature to be rude,
And all thy Kin full of Ingratitude,
I little thought thou wouldst presume so far,
To aim thy Malice at so bright a Star.

Now all the Service thou canst render me
Will never recompense this Injury.
Well, get thee gone for thou shalt never more
Have Power to hurt what I so much adore.
Hence from my Sight, and mayst thou ever lie
A crooked Object to each scornful Eye.

To Mrs. Harsenet, on the Report of a Beauty which she went to see at Church.

As when a Monarch does in Triumph come,
And proudly leads the vanquished Captive home,
The joyful People swarm in ev'ry Street,
And with loud Shouts the glorious Victor meet.

But others whom Misfortune kept away
Desire to hear the Story of the Day,
How brave the Prince, how brave his Chariot was,
How beautiful he look'd, with what a Grace;
How rich his Habit, if he Plumes did wear,
Or if a Wreath of Bays adorn'd his Hair:
They think 'twas wondrous fine, and long much more,
To see the Conqu'ror than they did before.

So when at first by Fame I only knew
The Charms so much admir'd and prais'd in you;
How many Slaves your conqu'ring Eyes had won,
And how the wond'ring Crowd did gazing throng;
I wish'd to see, and half a Lover grew,
Of so much Beauty, tho my Rival too.

I came, I saw you, and I must confess,
I wish'd my Beauty greater, or yours less;
Alas! My whole Devotion you betray'd,
I only thought of you, and only pray'd,
That you might all your jealous Sex out-do
In Cruelty as well as Beauty too.
I call'd Amintas faithless Man before,
But now I find 'tis just he should adore.
Not to love you, if such a Sin could be,
Were greater than his Perjury to me;
Thus while I blame him, I excuse him too,
Who can be innocent that looks on you?

But, lovely Chloris, you too meanly prize
The Treasures of your Youth, and of your Eyes;
Ne're hear his Vows that he to others swore,
Nor let him be your Slave, that was a Slave before;
He oft has Fetters worn, and can with Ease
Admit them, or dismiss them, as he please.
A Virgin Heart you merit, that ne're found
It could receive, till from your Eyes, a Wound,
The Soul that nothing but their Force could fear,
As great, if that can be, as you are fair.

For Damon, being ask'd a Reason for his Love.

I.
You ask me, Phillis why I still pursue,
And court no other Nymph but you;
And why with Looks and Sighs I still betray
A Passion which I dare not say.
'Tis all, Because I do: you ask me why,
And with a Woman's Reason, I reply.

II.
You ask what Argument I have to prove,
That my Unrest proceeds from Love,
You'll not believe my Passion till you know,
A better Reason why 'tis so.
Then, Phillis, let this Reason go for one,
I know I love because my Reason's gone.

III.

You say a Love like mine must needs declare
The Object so belov'd not fair;
That neither Wit nor Beauty in her dwell,
Whose Lover can no Reason tell,
What 'tis that he adores, and why he burns:
Phillis, let those give such that have returns.

IV.

And by the very Reasons that you use,
Damon might justly you accuse;
Why do you Scorn, and with a proud Disdain
Receive the Vow, and slight the Swain?
You say you cannot Love, you know no Cause:
May I not prove my Love by your own Laws?

V.

Am not I Youthful, and as gay a Swain,
As e'er appeared upon the Plain?
Have I not courted you with all th' Address
An am'rous Shepherd cou'd profess?
And add to this, my Flocks and Herds are great,
But Phillis only can my Joy compleat.

VI.

Yet you no Reason for your Coldness give,
And 'tis but just you shou'd believe
That all your Beauties unadorn'd by Art,
Have hurt and not oblig'd my Heart.
Be kind to that, my hearty Vows return
And then I'll tell you why, for what I burn.

FAMILIAR LETTERS, 1718.

A Letter to the Earl of Kildare, dissuading him from marrying Moll Howard.

My Lord,
We pity such as are by Tempest lost,
And those by Fortune's blind Disposal crost;
But when Men see, and may the Danger shun,
Yet headlong into certain Ruin run:
To pity such, must needs be Ridicule;
Do not (my Lord) be that unpity'd Fool.

There's a report, which round the Town is spread,
The fam'd Moll Howard you intend to Wed;
If it be true, my Lord, then guard your Head:

Horns, Horns, by wholesale, will adorn your Brows,
If e'r you make that rampant Whore your Spouse.
Think on the lewd Debauches of her Life;
Then tell me, if she's fit to be your Wife.
She that to quench her lustful, hot Desire,
Has Kiss'd with Dukes, Lords, Knights, and Country Squire;
Nay, Grooms and Footmen have been claw'd off by her.

Whoring has all her Life-time been her Trade,
And D—set says, she is an exc'lent Baud:
But finding both will not defray Expence,
She lately is become an Evidence;
Swears against all that won't her Lust supply,
And says, they're false as Hell to Monarchy.

You had a Wife; but, rest her Soul, she's dead,
By whom your Lordship by the Nose was led:
And will you run into that Noose agen,
To be the greatest Monster among Men?
Think on the Horns that will adorn your Head,
And the Diseases that will fill your Bed:
Pox upon Pox, most horrid and most dire!
And Ulcers filled with Hell's Eternal Fire.

Forbear therefore, and call your Senses home;
Let Reason Love's blind Passion overcome:
For, if you make this base Report once true,
You'l wound your Honour, Purse, and Body too.

To Mrs. Price.

My Dear,

In your last, you admir'd how I cou'd pass my Time so long in the Country: I am sorry your Taste is so deprav'd, as not to relish a Country-Life. Now I think there's no Satisfaction to be found amidst an Urban Throng (as Mr. Bayes calls it).

The peaceful Place where gladly I resort,
Is freed from noisy Factions of the Court:
There joy'd with viewing o'er the rural Scene,
Pleas'd with the Meadows ever green,
The Woods and Groves with tuneful Anger move,
And nought is heard but gentle Sighs of Love:
The Nymphs and Swains for rural Sports prepare,
And each kind Youth diverts his smiling Fair.
But if by Chance is found a flinty Maid,
Whose cruel Eyes has Shepherds Hearts betray'd,
In other Climes a Refuge she must find,
Banish'd from hence Society of Kind.

Here gentle Isis, with a Bridegroom's Haste,
Glides to o'ertake the Thame, as fair, as chaste;
Then mixt, embracing, they together flie;
They Live together, and together Die.
Here ev'ry Object adds to our Delight,
Calm is our Day, and peaceful is our Night.
Then, kind ^Emilia, flie that hated Town,
Where's not a Moment thou canst call thy own:
Haste for to meet a Happiness divine,
And share the Pleasures I count only mine.

P. S. A SONG.

I.
Tis not your saying that you love,
Can ease me of my Smart;
Your Actions must your Words approve,
Or else you break my Heart.

II.
In vain you bid my Passion cease,
And ease my troubled Breast;
Your Love alone must give me Peace,
Restore my wonted Rest.

III.
But, if I fail your Heart to move,
And 'tis not yours to give;
I cannot, wonnot cease to love,
But I will cease to live.

PROLOGUE to ROMULUS,

Spoken by Mrs. Butler.
Written by Mrs. Behn.

How we shall please ye now I cannot say;
But, Sirs, 'Faith here is News from Rome to day;
Yet know withal, we've no such PACKETS here,
As you read once a week from Monkey CARE.
But 'stead of that Lewd Stuff (that cloys the Nation)
Plain Love and Honour; (tho quite out of Fashion;)
Ours is a Virgin ROME, long, long, before
Pious GENEVA Rhetorick cail'd her Whore;
For be it known to their Eternal Shames,
Those Saints were always good at calling Names;
Of Scarlet Whores let 'em their Wills devise,

But let 'em raise no other Scarlet Lies;
LIES that advance the Good Old Cause, and bring
Into Contempt the PRELATES with the KING.
Why shou'd the Rebel Party be affraid?
They're Ratts and Weazles gnaw the Lyon's Beard,
And then in IGNORAMUS Holes they think,
Like other Vermin, to lie close, and stink.
What have ye got, ye Conscientious Knaves,
With all your Fancy 'd Power, and Bully Braves?
With all your standing to't; your Zealous Furies;
Your Lawless Tongues, and Arbitrary Juries?
Your Burlesque Oaths, when one Green-Ribbon-Brother
In Conscience will be Perjured for another?
Your PLOTS, Cabals, your Treats, Association,
Ye shame, ye very Nusance of the Nation,
What have ye got but one poor Word? Such Tools
Were Knaves before; to which you've added Fools.
Now I dare swear, some of you Whigsters say,
Come on, now for a swinging TORY PLAY.
But, Noble Whigs, pray let not those Fears start ye,
Nor fright hence any of the Sham Sheriff's Party;
For, if you'l take my censure of the Story,
It is as harmless as e're came before ye,
And writ before the times of Whig and Tory.

EPILOGUE to the Same.

Spoken by the Lady SLINGSBY.

Fair Ladies, pity an unhappy Maid,
By Fortune, and by faithless Love betray'd.
Innocent once I scarce knew how to sin,
Till that unlucky Devil entring in,
Did all my Honour, all my Faith undo:
LOVE! like Ambition makes us Rebels too:
And of all Treasons, mine was most accurst;
Rebelling 'gainst a KING and FATHER first.
A Sin, which Heav'n nor Man can e're forgive;
'Nor could I Act it with the Face to live.
My Dagger did my Honours cause redress;
But Oh! my blushing Ghost must needs confess,
Had my young Charming Lover faithful been,
I fear I dy'd with unrepented Sin.
There's nothing can my Reputation save
With all the True, the Loyal and the Brave;
Not my Remorse, or Death can expiate
With them a Treason 'gainst the KING and State.
Some Love-sick Maid perhaps, now I am gone,
(Raging with Love, and by that Love undone,)

May form some little Argument for me,
T' excuse m' Ingratitude and Treachery.
Some of the Sparks too, that infect the Pit,
(Whose Honesty is equal to their Wit,
And think Rebellion but a petty Crime,
Can turn to all sides Interest does incline,)
May cry 'I gad I think the Wench is wise;
'Had it proved Lucky, 'twas the Way to rise.
'She had a Roman Spirit, that disdains
'Dull Loyalty, and the Take of Sovereigns.
'A Pox of Fathers, and Reproach to come;
'She was the first and Noblest Whig of Rome.
But may that Ghost in quiet never rest,
Who thinks it self with Traytors Praises blest.

Mrs. Behn's Satyr on Dryden.
(On Mr. Dryden, Renegate.)

Scorning religion all thy life time past,
And now embracing popery at last,
Is like thyself; & what thou'st done before
Defying wife and marrying a whore.
Alas! how leering Hereticks will laugh
To see a gray old hedge bird caught with chaffe.
A Poet too from great heroick theames
And inspiration, fallen to dreaming dreams.
But this the priests will get by thee at least
That if they mend thee, miracles are not ceast.
For 'tis not more to cure the lame & blind,
Than heal an impious ulcerated mind.
This if they do, and give thee but a grain
Of common honesty, or common shame,
Twill be more credit to their cause I grant,
Than 'twould to make another man a saint.
But thou noe party ever shalt adorne,
To thy own shame & Nature's scandall borne:
All shun alike thy ugly outward part,
Whilest none have right or title to thy heart.
Resolved to stand & constant to the time,
Fix'd in thy lewdness, settled in thy crime.
Whilest Moses with the Israelites abode,
Thou seemdst content to worship Moses' God:
But since he went & since thy master fell,
Thou foundst a golden calf would do as well.
And when another Moses shall arise
Once more I know thou'lt rub and clear thy eyes,
And turn to be an Israelite again,
For when the play is done & fmisht clean,
What should the Poet doe but shift the scene.

VALENTINIAN.

Prologue spoken by Mrs. Cook the first Day.

Written by Mrs. Behn.

With that assurance we to day address,
As standard Beauties, certain of Success.
With careless Pride at once they charm and vex,
And scorn the little Censures of their Sex.
Sure of the unregarded Spoyl, despise
The needless Affectation of the Eyes,
The softening Languishment that faintly warms,
But trust alone to their resistless Charms.
So we secur'd by undisputed Wit,
Disdain the damning Malice of the Pit,
Nor need false Arts to set great Nature off,
Or studied tricks to force the Clap and Laugh.
Ye wou'd-be-Criticks, you are all undone,
For here's no Theam for you to work upon.
Faith seem to talk to Jenny y I advise,
Of who likes who, and how Loves Markets rise.
Try these hard Times how to abate the Price;
Tell her how cheap were Damsels on the Ice.
'Mongst City-Wives, and Daughters that came there,
How far a Guinny went at Blanket-Fair. The Fair on
Thus you may find some good Excuse for failing
Of your beloved Exercise of Railing.
That when Friend cryes How did the Play succeed?
Deme, I hardly minded what they did.
We shall not your Ill-nature please to day,
With some fond Scribblers new uncertain Play,
Loose as vain Youth, and tedious as dull Age,
Or Love and Honour that o're-runs the Stage.
Fam'd and substantial Authors give this Treat,
And 'twill be solemn, Noble all and Great.
Wit, sacred Wit, is all the bus'ness here;
Great Fletcher, and the greater Rochester.
Now name the hardy Man one fault dares find,
In the vast Work of two such Heroes joyn'd.
None but Great Strephons soft and pow'rful Wit
Durst undertake to mend what Fletcher writ,
Different their heav'nly Notes; yet both agree
To make an everlasting Harmony.
Listen, ye Virgins, to his charming Song,
Eternal Musick dwelt upon his Tongue.
The Gods of Love and Wit inspir'd his Pen,
And Love and Beauty was his glorious Theam.

Now, Ladies, you may celebrate his Name,
Without a scandal on your spotless Fame.
With Praise his dear lov'd Memory pursue,
And pay his Death, what to his Life was due.

To Henry Higden, Esq; on his Translation of the Tenth Satyr of Juvenal.

I.
I know you, and I must confess
From Sence so Celebrated, and so True,
Wit so Uncommon, and so New,
As that which alwaies shines in You;
I cou'd expect no less.
'Tis Great, 'tis Just, 'tis Noble all!
Right Spirit of the Original;
No scatter'd Spark, no glirhmering Beams,
As in some Pieces here and there,
Through a dark Glade of Duller Numbers gleams.
But tis all Fire! all Glittering every where
Grateful Instruction that can never fail,
To Please and Charm, even while you Rail.
By Arts thus Gentle and Severe
The Powers Divine first made their Mortals Wise;
The soft Reproach they did with Reverence bear;
While they Ador'd the GOD that did Chastize,

II.
Perhaps there may be found some Carping Wit,
May blame the Measures of thy Lines,
And cry, Not so the Roman Poet writ;
Who drest his Satyr in more lofty Rhimes.
But thou for thy Instructor Nature chose,
That first best Principle of Poetry;
And to thy Subject didst thy Verse dispose,
While in Harmonious Union both agree.
Had the Great Bard thy Properer Numbers view'd,
He wou'd have lay'd his stiff Heroicks by,
And this more Gay, more Airy Path pursu'd,
That so much better leads to Ralliery.
Wit is no more than Nature well exprest;
And he fatigues and toyles in vain
With Rigid Labours, breaks his Brain,
That has Familiar Thought in lofty Numbers drest.

III.
True to his Sense and to his Charming Wit,
Thou every where hast kept an equal Pace:
All his Brisk Turns exactly hit,
Justly maintain'd his Humour and his Grace:

And with the Language hast not chang'd the Face:
Great Juvenal in every Line,
True Roman still o're all does shine;
But in the Brittish Garb appears most fine.

IV.
Long did the Learned Author search to find
The Vice and Vanity of Humane-kind:
Long he observ'd, nor did observe in vain;
In every differing Humour found
Even there where Virtue did abound,
Some mortal Frailties reign.
Philosophers he saw were Proud
Of dull-affected Poverty:
Senators cringing to the Crowd
For trifling Popularity:
The Judge reviles the Criminal at Bar,
And now because old Ages Ice
Has chill'd the Ardour of his willing Vice,
Snarles at those Youthful Follies which he cannot shun,
From the vain-keeping 'Squire, and Cully'd Lord;
The fawning Courtier, States-man's Broken Word:
Down to the flattering, Jilting Curtizan,
And the more faithless couzening Citizen,
The Tricks of Court and State to him were known;
And all the Vices veil'd beneath the Gown,
From the Sharp Pulpit to the Blunted Stall,
He knew, and gently did reproach them all.

V.
If Rome that kept the lesser World in awe,
Wanted a Juvenal to give them Law,
How much more we who stockt with Knave and Fool,
Have turn'd the Nation into Ridicule.
The dire Contagion spreads to each degree
Of Wild Debauchery.
The mad Infected Youth make haste
To day their Fortunes, Health, and Reason waste:
The Fop, a tamer sort of Tool
Who dresses, talks, and loves, by Rule;
Has long for a Fine Person past.
Block-beads will pass for Wits, and Write,
And some for Brave, who ne'r could Fight.
Women for Chaste, whose knack of Cant
Boasts of the Virtues that they want:
Cry Faugh at Words and Actions Innocent,
And make that naughty that was never meant:
That vain-affected Hypocrite shall be
In Satyr sham'd to Honest Sense by Thee.
'Tis Thou, an English Juvenal, alone,
To whom all Vice, and every Venue's known:

Thou that like Judatfs King through all hast past,
And found that all's but Vanity at last;
'Tis you alone the Discipline can use,
Who dare at once be bold, severe, and kind;
Soften rough Satyr with thy gentler Muse,
And force a Blush at least, where you can't change the Mind.

How, to thy Sacred Memory, shall I bring
(Worthy thy Fame) a grateful Offering?
I, who by Toils of Sickness, am become
Almost as near as thou art to a Tomb?
While every soft, and every tender Strain
Is ruffl'd, and ill-natur'd grown with Pain.
But, at thy Name, my languisht Muse revives,
And a new Spark in the dull Ashes strives.
I hear thy tuneful Verse, thy Song Divine,
And am Inspired by every charming Line.
But, Oh!—
What Inspiration, at the second Hand,
Can an Immortal Elegie command?
Unless, like Pious Offerings, mine should be
Made Sacred, being Consecrate to thee.
Eternal, as thy own Almighty Verse,
Should be those Trophies that adorn thy Hearse.
The Thought Illustrious, and the Fancy young;
The Wit Sublime, the Judgment Fine and Strong;
Soft, as thy Notes to Sacharissa sung.
Whilst mine, like Transitory Flowers, decay,
That come to deck thy Tomb a short-liv'd Day.
Such Tributes are, like Tenures, only fit
To shew from whom we hold our Right to Wit.
Hail, wondrous Bard, whose Heav'n-born Genius first
My Infant Muse, and Blooming Fancy Nurst.
With thy soft Food of Love I first began,
Then fed on nobler Panegyrick Strain,
Numbers Seraphic! and at every View,
My Soul extended, and much larger grew:
Where e're I Read, new Raptures seiz'd my Blood;
Me thought I heard the Language of a God.

Long did the untun'd World in Ign'rance stray,
Producing nothing that was Great and Gay,
Till taught by thee, the true Poetick way.
Rough were the Tracts before, Dull and Obscure;
Nor Pleasure, nor Instruction could procure.
Their thoughtless Labour could no Passion move;
Sure, in that Age, the Poets knew not Love:

That Charming God, like Apparitions, then,
Was only talk'd on, but ne're seen by Men:
Darkness was o're the Muses Land displaid,
And even the Chosen Tribe unguided straid.
'Till, by thee rescu'd from th' Egyptian Night,
They now look up, and view the God of Light,
That taught them how to Love^ and how to Write ,
And to Enhance the Blessing which Heav'n lent,
When for our great Instructor thou wert sent,
Large was thy Life, but yet thy Glories more;
And, like the Sun, didst still dispense thy Pow'r,
Producing something wondrous ev'ry hour:
And in thy Circulary Course, didst see
The very Life and Death of Poetry.
Thou saw'st the Generous Nine neglected lie,
None listning to their Heav'nly Harmony;
The World being grown to that low Ebb of Sense
To disesteem the noblest Excellence;
And no Encouragement to Prophets shown,
Who in past Ages got so great Renown.
Though Fortune Elevated thee above
Its scanty Gratitude, or fickle Love;
Yet, sullen with the World, untir'd by Age,
Scorning th' unthinking Crowd, thou quit'st the Stage.

A PINDARIC POEM to the Reverend Doctor Burnet, on the Honour he did me of Enquiring after me
and my MUSE.

(I)
When Old Rome's Candidates aspir'd to Fame,
And did the Peoples Suffrages obtain
For some great Consul, or a Caesar's Name;
The Victor was not half so Pleas'd and Vain,
As I, when given the Honour of your Choice,
And Preference had in that one single Voice;
That Voice, from whence Immortal Wit still flows;
Wit that at once is Solemn all and Sweet,
Where Noblest Eloquence and Judgment shows
The Inspiring Mind Illustrious, Rich, and Great;
A Mind that can inform your wond'rous Pen
In all that's Perfect and Sublime:
And with an Art beyond the Wit of Men,
On what e're Theam, on what e're great Design,
It carries a Commanding Force, like that of Writ Divine.

(II)
With Pow'rful Reasoning drest in finest Sence,
A thousand ways my Soul you can Invade,
And spight of my Opinions weak Defence,

Against my Will, you Conquer and Perswade.
Your Language soft as Love, betrays the Heart,
And at each Period fixes a Resistless Dart,
While the fond Listner, like a Maid undone,
Inspired with Tenderness she fears to own;
In vain essays her Freedom to Regain:
The fine Ideas in her Soul remain,
And Please, and Charm, even while they Grieve and Pain.

(III)
But yet how well this Praise can Recompense
For all the welcome Wounds (before) you'd given!
Scarce any thing but You and Heaven
Such Grateful Bounties can dispense,
As that Eternity of Life can give;
So fam'd by you my Verse Eternally shall live:
Till now, my careless Muse no higher strove
T'inlarge her Glory, and extend her Wings;
Than underneath Parnassus Grove,
To Sing of Shepherds, and their humble Love;
But never durst, like Cowly, tune her Strings,
To sing of Heroes and of Kings.
But since by an Authority Divine,
She is allow'd a more exalted Thought;
She will be valu'd now as Currant Coyn;
Whose Stamp alone gives it the Estimate,
Tho' out of an inferiour Metal wrought.

(IV)
But oh! if from your Praise I feel
A Joy that has no Parallel!
What must I surfer when I cannot pay
Your Goodness, your own generous way?
And make my stubborn Muse your Just Commands obey.
My Muse that would endeavour fain to glide
With the fair prosperous Gale, and the full driving Tide,
But Loyalty Commands with Pious Force,
That stops me in the thriving Course,
The Brieze that wafts the Crowding Nations o're,
Leaves me unpity'd far behind
On the Forsaken Barren Shore,
To Sigh with Echo, and the Murmuring Wind;
While all the Inviting Prospect I survey,
With Melancholy Eyes I view the Plains,
Where all I see is Ravishing and Gay,
And all I hear is Mirth in loudest Strains;
Thus while the Chosen Seed possess the Promis'd Land,
I like the Excluded Prophet stand,
The Fruitful Happy Soil can only see,
But am forbid by Fates Decree
To share the Triumph of the joyful Victory.

(V)

'Tis to your Pen, Great Sir, the Nation owes
For all the Good this Mighty Change has wrought;
'Twas that the wondrous Method did dispose,
E're the vast Work was to Perfection brought.
Oh Strange effect of a Seraphick Quill!
That can by unperceptable degrees
Change every Notion, every Principle
To any Form, its Great Dictator please:
The Sword a Feeble Pow'r, compar'd to That,
And to the Nobler Pen subordinate;
And of less use in Bravest turns of State:
While that to Blood and Slaughter has recourse,
This Conquers Hearts with soft prevailing Force:
So when the wiser Greeks o'recame their Foes,
It was not by the Barbarous Force of Blows.
When a long Ten Years Fatal War had fail'd,
With luckier Wisdom they at last assail'd,
Wisdom and Counsel which alone prevaiPd.
Not all their Numbers the Fam'd Town could win,
'Twas Nobler Stratagem that let the Conquerour in.

(VI)

Tho' I the Wond'rous Change deplore,
That makes me Useless and Forlorn,
Yet I the great Design adore,
Tho' Ruin'd in the Universal Turn.
Nor can my Indigence and Lost Repose,
Those Meagre Furies that surround me close,
Convert my Sense and Reason more
To this Unpresidented Enterprise,
Than that a Man so Great, so Learn'd, so Wise,
The Brave Atchievement Owns and nobly Justifies.
'Tis you, Great Sir, alone, by Heaven preserved,
Whose Conduct has so well the Nation serv'd,
'Tis you that to Posperity shall give
This Ages Wonders, and its History.
And Great NASSAU shall in your Annals live
To all Futurity.
Your Pen shall more Immortalize his Name,
That even his Own Renown'd and Celebrated Fame.

APHRA BEHN – A SHORT BIOGRAPHY

Aphra Behn was baptised on December 14th in 1640.

Although she was a prolific and well established writer in her own lifetime facts about her remain scant and difficult to confirm. What can safely be said though is that Aphra Behn is now regarded as a key English playwright and a major figure in Restoration theatre

In fact even where and to whom she was born are subject to discussion.

According to which account you read – and there are many – Aphra was born in Harbledown, near Canterbury. Another that she was born to a barber, John Amis and his wife Amy. Or again she was born to a couple named Cooper.

In the "The Histories And Novels of the Late Ingenious Mrs. Behn" (1696) it is written that Aphra was born to Bartholomew Johnson, a barber, and Elizabeth Denham, a wet-nurse. However a claim by Colonel Thomas Colepeper, who states he knew her as a child, wrote in Adversaria that she was born at "Sturry or Canterbury" to a Mr Johnson and that she had a sister named Frances. Anne Kingsmill Finch, Countess of Winchilsea, a poetic contemporary, says that Aphra was born in Wye in Kent, and was the 'Daughter to a Barber.'

None of these accounts can be relied upon and it follows that with so few facts the early part of her life cannot be clearly illustrated.

However what can be accurately suggested is that Aphra was born in the rising tensions to the English Civil War. Obviously a time of much division and difficulty as the King and Parliament, and their respective forces, came ever closer to conflict.

But still facts do not reveal themselves in any quantity. As a young woman a version exists of Aphra's journeying to Surinam with Bartholomew Johnson. He was said to have died on the journey, leaving his wife and children spending some months in the country. It is during this trip that Aphra claims to have met an African slave leader. These experiences formed the basis for one of her most famous works, "Oroonoko". In "Oroonoko" Behn Aphra gifts herself the position of narrator and her first biographer accepted the proposition that Aphra was indeed the daughter of the lieutenant general of Surinam, as in the story. There is little evidence to support this case, and none of her contemporaries acknowledge this, or any, aristocratic status. There is also no evidence that Oroonoko existed as an actual person or that any such slave revolt, is anything but an invention.

However it is possible that she acted a spy in the colony. Possibilities exist. Perhaps Aphra re-wrote her own history as and when it suited her needs at the time.

The common method of gathering information in these times was Church records and for a few, tax records. Aphra Behn is mentioned in neither. As well as Aphra Behn or Mrs Behn she was, at times, also known as Ann Behn, Mrs Bean, agent 160 and Astrea.

Shortly after her supposed return to England from Surinam in 1664, Aphra may have married Johan Behn (also written as Johann and John Behn). He could have been a merchant of German or Dutch extraction, possibly from Hamburg. He died or the couple separated that same year, however from this point we can be sure Aphra used the title "Mrs Behn" as her professional name.

There is some suggestion that Aphra may have been a Catholic or at least leaned towards this school of faith. She once commented that she was "designed for a nun." Many of those around her were Catholic, such as Henry Neville who was later arrested for his Catholicism, and this would have aroused suspicions during the anti-Catholic fervour of the 1680s. She was a monarchist, and her sympathy for the Stuarts, and particularly for the Catholic Duke of York may be demonstrated by her dedication of her play "The Rover, Part II" to him after he had been exiled for the second time. Aphra was dedicated to the restored King Charles II. As political parties emerged during this time, Aphra became a Tory supporter.

By 1666 Aphra had become attached to the court. Domestically the Plague was sweeping the Nation and the Great Fire was about to erupt through London. In foreign affairs England and the Netherlands had engaged in The Second Anglo-Dutch War from 1665. Aphra was recruited as a political spy in Antwerp on behalf of King Charles II, possibly in league with Thomas Killigrew.

This is probably the beginning of more accurate records on Aphra's life. Her code name is said to have been Astrea (though there are others), a name under which she later published many of her writings. Her chief duty was to establish a relationship with William Scot, son of Thomas Scot, a regicide who had been executed in 1660. Scot was believed to be ready to become a spy in the English service and to report on the activities of the English exiles who were thought to be plotting against the King. Aphra arrived in Bruges in July 1666 with a mission to secure Scot into a double agent, but there is evidence that Scot would betray her to the Dutch.

Aphra however found life as a spy not quite the romantic interlude that many assume would be the case. She arrived unprepared; the cost of living shocked her, and after a month, she had to pawn her jewellery. King Charles was slow in paying, either for her services or for her expenses whilst abroad. She had to borrow money so she could return to London, where she spent a year petitioning King Charles for payment unsuccessfully. A short while later a warrant was issued for her arrest, but little to suggest it was actually served or that she went to prison for her debt.

The death of her husband and her debts seemed to push her towards a more sustainable and substantial career. Aphra began work for the King's Company and the Duke's Company players as a scribe. These were, in fact, the only two licensed theatre groups in London. The theatres had been closed under Cromwell and were now re-opening under Charles II and a more liberal atmosphere. Theatre technology was being imported from Europe and being integrated into the staging of some plays. It was a great moment on which to embark upon a career in theatre.

Aphra who had previously only written poetry now embarked on such a career. Her first, "The Forc'd Marriage", was staged in 1670, followed by "The Amorous Prince" (1671). After her third play, "The Dutch Lover", fails to please Aphra had a three year lull in her writing career. Again it is speculated that she went travelling again, possibly once again as a spy.

After this sojourn her writing moves towards comic works, which prove commercially more successful. Her most popular works included "The Rover" and "Love-Letters Between a Nobleman and His Sister" (1684–87).

With her growing reputation Aphra became friends with many of the most notable writers of the day. This is The Age of Dryden and his literary dominance. As well as his friendship she includes also those of Elizabeth Barry, John Hoyle, Thomas Otway and Edward Ravenscroft, and was also attached to the circle of the Earl of Rochester.

Aphra often used her plays to attack the parliamentary Whigs claiming, "In public spirits call'd, good o' th' Commonwealth... So tho' by different ways the fever seize...in all 'tis one and the same mad disease." This was Aphra's criticism to parliament which had denied the king funds.

From the mid 1680's Aphra's health began to decline. This was exacerbated by her continual state of debt and descent into poverty.

In 1687 she published A Discovery of New Worlds, a translation of a French popularisation of astronomy, Entretiens sur la pluralité des mondes, by Bernard le Bovier de Fontenelle, written as a novel in a form similar to her own work, but with her new, religiously oriented preface.

As her end approached in 1689 it became increasingly hard for her to even hold a pen though her desire to continue to write was unquenchable. In her final days, she wrote the translation of the final book of Abraham Cowley's Six Books of Plants.

Aphra Behn died on April 16th 1689, and is buried in the East Cloister of Westminster Abbey. The inscription on her tombstone reads: "Here lies a Proof that Wit can never be Defence enough against Mortality." She was quoted as stating that she had led a "life dedicated to pleasure and poetry."

Her legacy is broad. Firstly as a woman she broke down many of the barriers which regarded only men as writers, especially in the commercial arena. In all she would write and have performed 19 plays, contribute to more, and become one of the first prolific, high-profile female dramatists in these Isles.

In her own golden age of the 1670s and 1680s she was one of the most productive playwrights in Britain, second only to the immense talents of the Poet Laureate John Dryden.

Much of her work has been criticised for its bawdy tone as well as its masculine form but needs must and she was working to live, to survive, and to widen her spread as an author.

She received widespread support from many other successful writers including Thomas Otway, Nahum Tate (also a Poet Laureate), Jacob Tonson, Nathaniel Lee and Thomas Creech.

Aphra is now rightly seen as a key dramatist of the seventeenth-century theatre. Her prose vitally important to the on-going development of the English novel.

Following Aphra's death new female dramatists such as 'Ariadne', Delarivier Manley, Mary Fix, Susanna Centlivre and Catherine Trotter acknowledged Behn as an inspiration who opened up the public space for women writers to be accepted.

In succeeding centuries her appreciation has been volatile. For instance in the morally reserved Victorian clime both the writer and her works were ignored or dismissed as indecent. The Victorian novelist and critic Julia Kavanagh wrote, "the disgrace of Aphra Behn is that, instead of raising man to woman's moral standard, she sank woman to the level of man's coarseness".

However by the 20th century, however, Aphra's fame was back in fashion. Since then her works have been well appreciated and her place in our literary pantheon assured.

APHRA BEHN – A CONCISE BIBLIOGRAPHY

Plays
The Forced Marriage (1670)
The Amorous Prince (1671)
The Dutch Lover (1673)
Abdelazer (1676)

The Town Fop (1676)
The Rover, Part I (1677)
Sir Patient Fancy (1678)
The Feigned Courtesans (1679)
The Young King (1679)
The False Count (1681)
The Rover, Part II (1681)
The Roundheads (1681)
The City Heiress (1682)
Like Father, Like Son (1682)
Prologue and Epilogue to Romulus and Hersilia, or The Sabine War (November 1682)
The Lucky Chance (1686) with composer John Blow
The Emperor of the Moon (1687)
The Widow Ranter (1689)
The Younger Brother (1696)

Novels
The Fair Jilt
Agnes de Castro
Love-Letters Between a Nobleman and His Sister (1684)
Oroonoko (1688)

Short Stories
The Fair Jilt (1688)
The History of the Nun: or, the Fair Vow-Breaker (1688)
The History of the Servant
The Lover-Boy of Germany
The Girl Who Loved the German Lover-Boy

Poetry Collections
Poems upon Several Occasions, with A Voyage to the Island of Love (1684)
Lycidus; or, The Lover in Fashion (1688)